SAILING BOATS

RACING AND REGATTAS

With an introduction by Nico Rode

**ORBIS BOOKS
LONDON**

Contents

The colour photographs in this book were supplied by:
Alpa: 39; Barka: 36, 38; Beken of Cowes: 31, 47; C Bevilacqua:
2, 3; MB: 75; Cima: 30; Conti: 19; G Costa: 4, 28, 54, 58;
M. Gallini: 41; Nautica Visnara: 40; Neptune Nautisme: 32, 44;
Ostman/Dahlin: 25; P Popper: 46; B Richner: 1, 13–15, 21, 23,
37, 42; N Rode: 5–8, 11, 17, 18, 22, 24, 26, 27, 29, 33, 34, 49–53,
55–57, 59–74; L Sirman: 20; Sparks Marine: 35; Time Life: 43
(G Silk) 48 (M Manney); Transworld/G Granham: 45;
Yeldham/Studio 77: 10; A & G Zampa: 9; ZFA: 12, 16.

Translated and adapted by Anthony Churchill

© Istituto Geografico de Agostini, Novara 1968
English edition © Orbis Publishing Limited, London 1973
Phototypeset in England by Petty and Sons Limited, Leeds
Printed in Italy by IGDA, Novara
ISBN 0 85613 138 5

This is a book for everyman. For the learner, here are numerous diagrams and explanations about yachts and their handling; for the expert, here are technical photographs and captions to refresh the memory, and give fresh slants to what might be already known; for the dreamer, here are superb colour photographs, on almost every page, to show you the whole range of boats which eventually you may wish to buy. Come and join us in this sport of kings, now enjoyed by millions – whether as a racing or a cruising man, a 'big boat' yachtie or a small dinghy fanatic. Modern methods of production have brought down the cost of this leisure pursuit until it comes within the grasp of the majority. But first, look through these pages and find out in what direction you should move.

To start with, this book examines the vocabulary of yachting. We take a look at the hull, sails, and at simple manoeuvres. Then we take you into the realm of racing. Racing is a vital part of yachting, for there you may learn at close quarters what makes the boat sail, and what makes her sail fast. Finally, you may even get to the toughest competition and enter international races. At the peak is the Olympic Games. In these pages you will find a description of many racing dinghies and keelboats, and there is a detailed description of the six types of boat now allowed into the Olympics. A number of pages are devoted to the more sophisticated tactics which you would find in such a competition. As for the big boats, a major event which gains the headlines is the Americas Cup, won every time since the last century by the Americans, and a target for ambitious men overseas – especially those from France and Australia.

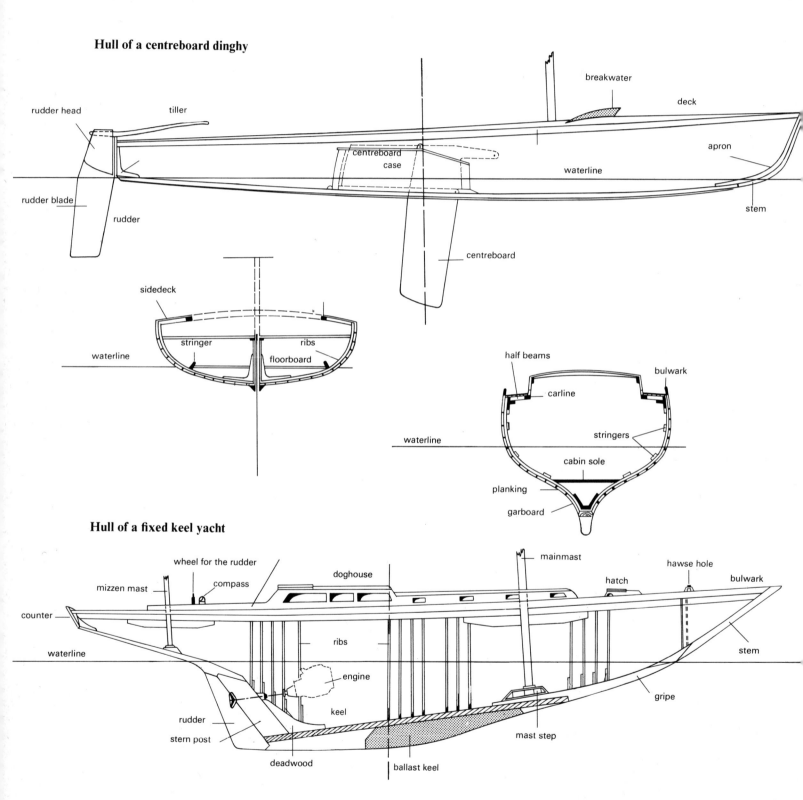

Hull of a centreboard dinghy

rudder head

tiller

breakwater

deck

apron

centreboard case

waterline

rudder blade

rudder

stem

centreboard

sidedeck

stringer

ribs

waterline

floorboard

half beams

bulwark

carline

stringers

waterline

cabin sole

planking

garboard

Hull of a fixed keel yacht

wheel for the rudder

mainmast

hawse hole

doghouse

hatch

bulwark

mizzen mast

compass

counter

ribs

stem

waterline

engine

rudder

keel

gripe

stern post

mast step

deadwood

ballast keel

4

An introduction to sailing

Modern methods of construction, and especially the use of glass reinforced plastics (glassfibre), have allowed builders to produce boat hulls in series. Thus naval architects and builders can produce at lower cost, and this has opened out the boating world to an ever-growing number of newcomers, and especially to those with limited budgets. Thanks to recent developments it has become possible to make larger boats in glassfibre, even up to medium and large cruisers. This has contributed dramatically to what we know as the 'boom' in boating. If you watch as boats navigate along our coastlines, or sail serenely across lakes and inland seas, you can see that the scope is there for even more people to take up this sport, although it must also be said that ports are often crowded. This situation is being alleviated slowly by the construction of many new marinas all over the world.

In this book I have tried, as far as I can, to represent the great variety of boats which are available. The old belief that boating is a sport only for the rich is no longer true. There is now a boat suited to every man's income.

In writing about sailing boats I have not been able to avoid discussing racing, or sailing regattas. From my experience I have known many, many people who have bought a boat only for some gentle cruising, but they have soon become addicted to racing. It is not difficult to understand why the bug catches on, for when two boats are on the same course it is difficult for one not to try to pass the other. That is how an interest in racing starts.

Controlling a sailing boat, and navigating it properly, is not difficult to learn; but to get the very best out of a boat, to perfect your knowledge of the whole sport and to put it into practice, and to get up to world championship standards, demands – as do all sports – complete dedication, constant practice, concentration and determination.

There are many schools where you can learn sailing, especially for the young, but there are some for men and women of all ages. As I have had the privilege of running a course on sailing I have been able to see at first hand the enthusiasm with which newcomers greet their new sport, and the care with which they study the basics of seamanship.

I personally hope that boating will become more and more the means by which people can escape from the stresses and strains of modern society. Sailing on peaceful lakes or on the sea, listening only to the lapping of waves breaking on the hull, I hope they may find the relaxation and calm which is so necessary to counteract the breakneck pace of today.

The hull

Every type of boat, whether it has oars, sails, or an engine, has a floating body which is under pressure from a force acting in a downwards direction (the hydrostatic force) equal to the weight of the liquid that it displaces. For sailing boats, the name of the 'floating body' is the hull, and this supports the weight of the crew, the weight of the mast and rigging, and of the ballast. The shape of the hull and its characteristics are studied carefully and, depending on what the hull is to be used for, it will be drawn up by a naval architect or designer. It is he who calculates all the problems of the boat's stability, its behaviour in a seaway, its ability to cut through the water, and in the special case of racing boats, its centreboard and its resistance (lateral displacement caused by the wind and sea).

The part of the hull which is below the waterline is the bottom of the boat, and the part of the hull above the waterline is called the topsides.

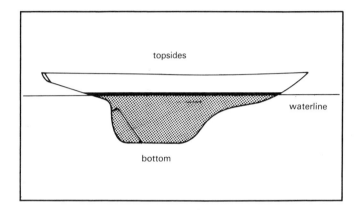

You can, in general, divide types of hull into two categories:
1. Hulls with round bilges (those with their transverse sections rounded);
2. Hulls with a hard chine (those with their transverse section angled).
Usually these latter have a single chine (one angle either side), or they may be double chined (with two angles either side).

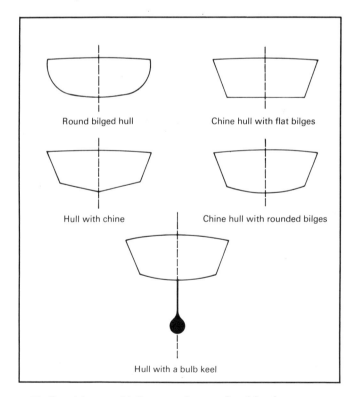

Round bilged hull

Chine hull with flat bilges

Hull with chine

Chine hull with rounded bilges

Hull with a bulb keel

Hulls with round bilges can have a fixed keel, or a moveable keel which retracts into the hull, variously called a drop keel, centreboard, or dagger plate. Hulls with a hard chine can have bilges shaped in a V, or they can be flat or rounded.

Hulls with a fixed keel carry in their lower part a weight, called ballast, made usually of lead or iron. This ballast may be carried inside the hull itself, but these days it usually forms the bottom part of the keel; or it may be made into an aerodynamic bulb or blister, and fixed onto the bottom of the keel. This ballast counteracts the force of the wind, which will tend to push into the sails, and thus the mast and hull, sideways towards the water.

Hulls with bulb keels are a part of the category of hulls with fixed keels. These boats can be flat or round bilged, and on the bottom of their hull is fixed a plate, usually in cast iron, carrying at its lowest part a weight elongated into the shape of a bulb with good hydrodynamic qualities.

Hulls with lifting keels are usually found in boats which are light, without very tall masts and with a fairly small sail area; those, even without ballast, have a positive amount of stability owing to their wide, flat shape. In small boats of this type the crewman leans outboard and uses his own weight to counteract the force of the wind on the sails.

A boat leans sideways (heels) because of the force of the wind on her side, but this wind also causes her to slip sideways through the water slightly (to have leeway). For a fixed keel boat this leeway is lessened by the shape of the hull and keel, which are usually quite deeply submerged. For small boats, the resistance to this sideways movement is made by the drop keel (which is usually made of wood or metal). The drop keel can be retracted into the hull.

A drop keel can either pivot around a metal rod at its front, or it may lift up and down. The former is called a centreboard, the latter a dagger plate. The centreboard is fixed in its front part (low down) and it pivots around this axis, swinging down into the water. A system of blocks or pulleys enables it to be pulled up into the centreboard case, where it is fully retracted out of the water. The dagger plate has a far shorter housing, since it does not swing its length upwards into the boat – it is lifted vertically upwards (or nearly vertically upwards). When it is raised, its upper part shows above its housing.

The rudder

The keel and the drop-keel are used to act in opposition to the lateral forces of the wind and the sea. If you wish to sail forwards in a certain direction, or to change your course, then you have to use a rudder. This is a thin blade, fixed in small sailing boats onto the back (transom) in such a manner that it may be moved as a door moves on its hinges. It has a solid head, into which fits the tiller, which is held by the helmsman. The rudder has a lower part, or rudder blade, which is in contact with the water. The rudder is fixed by vertical pins (attached to the rudder itself and called pintles) which engage into gudgeons (which are fixed to the transom). The rudder can be in one piece, or it can be a lifting rudder, in which case the blade pivots upwards and out of the water. Though the rudder is fixed on the back end of the boat in small craft, in bigger boats it is usually fixed underneath the waterline, aft of the keel. It may be fixed onto a piece of wood in

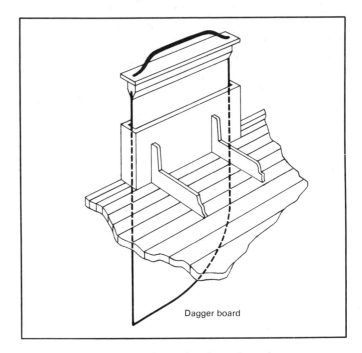

Dagger board

front of it (the skeg), or it can jut down into the water on its own. A near-vertical shaft runs from the top of the rudder through the hull, where it is fixed to a tiller, or to a wheel.

Mast and rigging

The force of the wind acts on the sails, and they transmit their power to the boat by means of the rigging. The

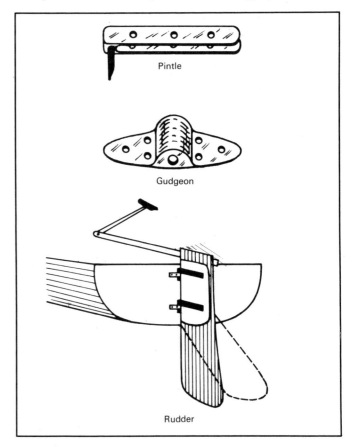

Pintle

Gudgeon

Rudder

rigging is composed of the mast, other spars (a boom, gaff), stays and shrouds, and a number of moving wires and ropes necessary to keep the sails in place, which you have to alter according to the wind's direction and force. There are many types of rig, but the one which we will concentrate on is called the Marconi or Bermuda rig. It is the most common one in the world today, especially in modern yachts.

In the rigging, you can separate out the fixed rigging from the running rigging. The fixed rigging consists of the shrouds, the forestay and backstay and other wires which hold up the mast. The running rigging is all those pieces of rope or wire rope which move, and which are used to raise or lower sails, to stretch them out, or to ease them out. You have to alter the position of these ropes depending on the amount of wind there is to sail with, and where the wind is coming from. The halyards are used to hoist the sails or lower them, depending on the amount of wind; the sheets are used to ease the sails out and in, but mainly to adjust them to take account of where the wind is coming from.

The halyards run up the mast and round sheaves fixed near the top of the mast (for mainsails and jibs), though for some jibs the sheave may be fixed about three quarters of the way up the mast. The halyards are fixed onto cleats and jam cleats near the bottom of the mast. On bigger yachts, they may be held by winches and cleats.

The jib sheets go round pulleys or jib leads fixed on the deck. The mainsail sheet runs round a series of blocks fixed both on the boom and on the deck, or on a metal bar (the horse) running above the transom.

The sails

Usually a sailing boat has two basic sails (singlehanded dinghies, though, usually only have one sail). These sails are triangular, one in front of the mast (the jib) and the other one aft of the mast (the mainsail). The mainsail is hoisted vertically up the back part of the mast, and stretched horizontally out along the boom.

The jib, which has its front part stitched around a wire rope, can be hoisted without any attachment except at the bottom (the tack); or it has hanks (metal or plastic clips) which are engaged around the forestay, and this allows the sail to be hoisted close to this forestay. The mainsail is, as its name suggests, the principal sail. It too is sewn around a rope, along its leading edge (or luff). The part of the sail that goes along the boom is called the foot of the sail. The longest length of the sail, which goes from the head of the mast out to the end of the boom, is called the leech. The leech carries two or three pockets of cloth sewn into the sail, and into these you place long, thin, flexible pieces of wood, called battens, which are there to keep the leech from falling in.

The action of wind on sail pushes the boat forward, and the choice of which sails to hoist in different wind conditions is most important for racing boats. The shape of the sail is vital. When there is a flat calm, or when there is only a small amount of wind, you can use a 'full' sail to get the best speed from your boat. In winds between 10 and 20 knots, an average shaped sail will be best suited to the conditions. If the wind is more than 20 knots, then a

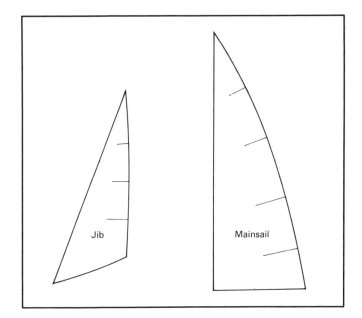

Jib | Mainsail

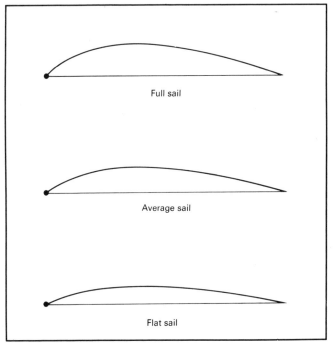

Full sail

Average sail

Flat sail

flat sail will certainly be best when going to windward, as it will cause the boat to heel over rather less. You have a problem, however, for the wind can easily slacken its strength during the course of a race, or it can suddenly blow. What sail should you then use, knowing a 'full' sail is good for little wind, and a 'flat' sail for plenty of wind? Sails with less fullness will generally sail better than sails with greater fullness, for if the wind becomes stronger it is easy, by bending the mast and the boom, to flatten the sail without changing it. In these new conditions, a boat with full sails will have difficulty in using her mast-bend to 'flatten' her sails completely.

The spinnaker is a huge sail with a semi-spherical shape, made in very light cloth, and it is hoisted when the wind is free, i.e. when the wind is across the boat, or coming from behind. This sail can increase the boat's speed remarkably. The shape of spinnakers has changed considerably; they used to be even more spherical. Their hoisting and setting is rather the same as for a jib. They can sometimes be used when the wind is abeam or just ahead of abeam. When the wind is astern, the spinnaker pole can be carried as far away from the bow as possible, so that the sail presents as much area as it can to the wind, without being shadowed from the wind by the mainsail. In a light breeze, the spinnaker pole may be carried low down the mast and at right angles to it. If the wind starts to rise, and the spinnaker billows out, you can put the spinnaker pole higher up the mast.

To get the best results from your spinnaker in winds above 8 and 10 knots, ease out the halyard by a few inches in small boats, or more for cruising boats, according to the strength of the wind. In a weak breeze, the spinnaker must be hoisted right up, and stretched out to a maximum.

The setting of sails

Setting your sails correctly is most important, if you wish to get the best speed out of your boat, especially when you come to the setting of the jib in relation to the mainsail. There are many places to which the sheet of the jib can be led to get different results.

If a jib is set too open by comparison with the 'set' of the mainsail, it creates wind eddies and disperses the wind behind the mainsail. A jib set too tightly will direct the shafts of wind onto the back of the mainsail, 'backwinding' it. The ideal shape of the jib is achieved when the profile of the sail follows, along its length, that of the back of the mainsail, in such a way that the shafts of wind run parallel.

The choice of where you attach the sheet of the jib is not an easy one and it depends on the type of boat. The large 12 metres attach their jib sheet at an angle of 7 degrees to the fore-and-aft line of the boat. The Star has points to which you may attach the jib at 10 degrees and 11 degrees. The 5.5 metre class can angle the jib at 10 degrees and 10.5 degrees. This angle varies, for most other boats, between 10 degrees and 14 degrees. The big cruising yachts have tracks at different angles, running towards the bow, and this enables you to alter the sheet lead as you like.

You have to angle your jib to the fore and aft line: you must also decide how far for'ard or aft to sheet it. The sheet's lead will be placed so that the pull on the sail is as nearly as possible at right angles to the forestay. If you find that your sail is bulging up high, then the sheet must be led further forward. If the back end (leech) is too tight, then the sheet must be led further aft.

The wind

The wind is the only means of propelling a boat forward allowed to a sail boat, and specifically rule 60 of the IYRU (International Yacht Racing Union) begins 'A yacht shall be propelled only by the natural action of the wind on the sails, spars and hull, and water on the hull'.

A sailing boat has the wind 'free' when it has the wind moving in the same path, or nearly so, as the direction in which the boat is going. On this point of sailing, the hull

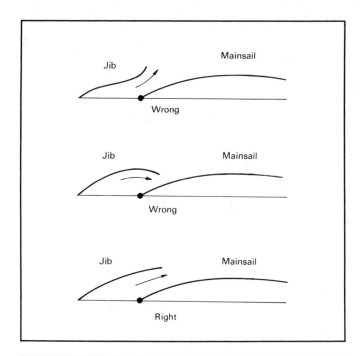

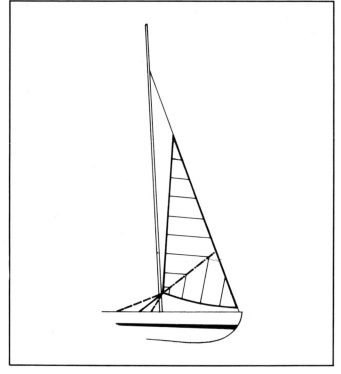

will not have any lateral displacement, and the centreboard is raised to increase the speed of the boat. Sheets are eased right out, and spinnakers are hoisted. This point of sailing will appear to be easy to sail, but in fact complications multiply when the wind breezes up and when high seas are running. Then the boat becomes a delicate and dangerous instrument, to be sailed with care. Correct manoeuvres are important if the mast is to stay in the boat, and indeed if the boat is to remain upright. A boat sailing on a 'reach' has the wind blowing across her, and the tendency is for her to fall off to leeward. In this case, the keel or centreboard is lowered into the water and there it acts against the pressure of the wind,

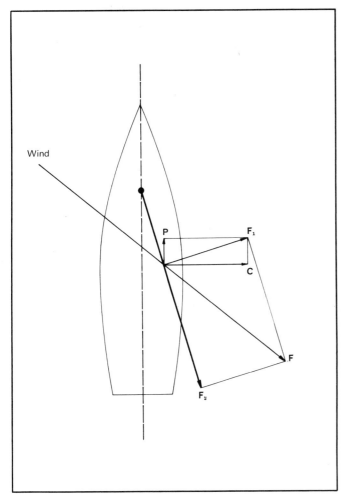

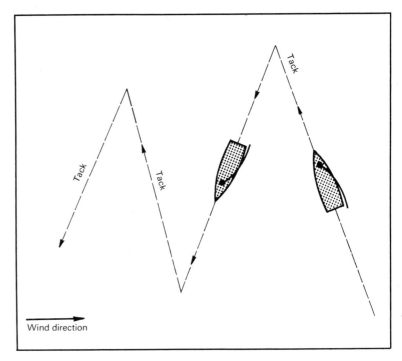

helping to keep the boat upright. This point of sailing is the fastest for sailing boats. It does not pose any particular problem, and once the boat is on her proper course, the sheets can be positioned in such a way that the sails set well, without one interfering with the other.

The last point of sailing, which is a mystery to many people, is 'on the wind'. A sailing boat cannot point straight into the wind, for the sails will simply flap (or slat). To enable a boat to reach a point straight into the eye of the wind, it has to follow a zig-zag course, the fore-and-aft line of the boat making an angle to the wind, with the wind first on one side then on the other and the sails filling. This broken line which the boat must follow is called a tack to windward, or a course dead to windward. Modern racing boats point at an angle of less than 40 degrees to the direction of the wind. On this windward point of sailing, the keel or centreboard has the most important part to play, and must be completely lowered.

This phenomenon of a boat sailing to windward can partly be explained in a diagram. Force F which is acting on the sails of the boat is in fact composed of two other forces. F1 is the force perpendicular to the boom, and F2 is the force parallel to the boom. F2 has the effect of a brake on the boat's progress, while in its turn Force F is composed of two forces, Force C, perpendicular to the path of the boat, and Force P, acting in the same direction as the boat. It is the small component P which is giving the boat its forward motion on this point of sailing. Force

C tends to heel the boat and even to turn it over. Against this force is opposed the stability caused by the shape of the hull, and the ballast in the keel of the boat, as well as the weight of the crewmen who, as moveable ballast, are moved up to windward, either by leaning out (sitting out) over the side of the boat, or by using a trapeze. Because a boat is designed to sail better when her hull is upright, it is preferable to prevent her from heeling over excessively.

The three points of sailing which we have just looked at are the main ones, but there are other intermediate points of sailing. On any point of sailing it is necessary to find an equilibrium. When a boat is fully 'tuned', it should be able to make any point of sailing without having to use the rudder: then indeed the boat is in equilibrium.

Thus you must get the centre of effort of the sails and the centre of effort of the hull in phase with each other. If the perpendicular passing through the centre of effort of the sails is ahead of the centre of effort of the hull, the boat will have lee helm (and she will have a tendency to bear away), and if the centre of effort of the sails is behind that of the hull, then she will have a tendency to have weather helm (or to luff up).

You can get equilibrium in your boat by making small adjustments to her, by changing the position, for example, of the point where the jib is tacked down, either forward or aft. When the boat has too much weather helm (this is a common ailment) you may have to put the mast further back; if the boat has too much lee helm, you may have to put the mast somewhat forward.

Manoeuvres

To luff (or luff up) signifies that the boat is changing course towards the direction from which the wind is coming. To bear off, or to sail freer, is to change the course of the boat away from the direction of the wind, and so it is the exact opposite of 'to luff up'.

Starboard tack: a yacht is said to be on starboard tack

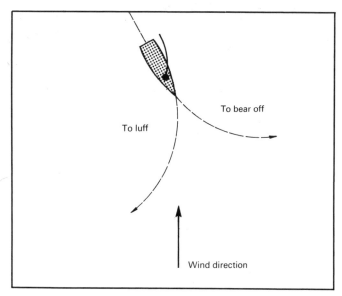

To bear off

To luff

Wind direction

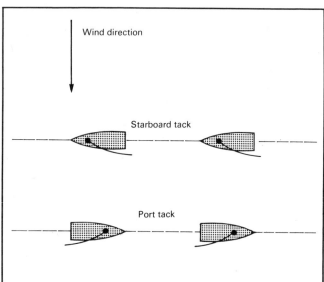

Wind direction

Starboard tack

Port tack

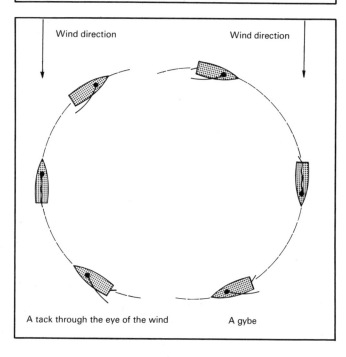

Wind direction

Wind direction

A tack through the eye of the wind

A gybe

when it feels the wind coming from the right hand side of the boat.

Port tack: a boat is on port tack when it feels the wind coming from the left hand side.

To change tacks – to tack, or go about: this is the manoeuvre you have to follow to get a boat from port to starboard tack, and vice versa. If you make the manoeuvre when close hauled, the bows of the boat pass through the eye of the wind, and you are indeed tacking or going about. But if you are sailing free, on a reach or a run, and you turn the boat's stern through the wind, then you are gybing.

In case of damage, or even to get out to the starting line when there is no wind, it may be necessary to take a tow. The boat may be towed by a fast motor boat or a slow workboat. In both cases the towing boat must let out a main cable to which may be attached subsidiary lines which the towed boat may pick up (see diagram). It is important that the knot fixing it to the main towing wire (which can be either single or double) has a shackle so that the minor wire may be easily disengaged. This is because the tension and the dragging of the wire through the water may make it necessary to let go of the whole of the tow quickly in case of danger. It is also wise to try and get an even pull, so boats of the same type should be, where possible, attached near to each other on either side of the tow, and with the points of attachment as near as possible. This allows one boat to get near to the point of attachment and to let go the lead of another boat, and then to let go its own. The line of the tow must be as straight as possible to avoid the breakages and collisions which can result from a moment of inattention. The towing line must not be too long – 7 to 10 yards are sufficient. It is preferable to moor the line to the foot of the mast, after protecting this first with a sailbag or cloth.

During the tow, you must follow carefully the manoeuvres of the towing boat, and be attentive in case the tow takes charge or breaks.

Classification of racing boats

The types of racing boat which are most important and have the widest popularity throughout the world are those which are built according to the rules of the International Yacht Racing Union, known by the initials IYRU, which has its headquarters in London. It is the greatest world authority in sailing, and it controls all the international rules and competitions. Some nations also have their own series of races, controlled by their own national

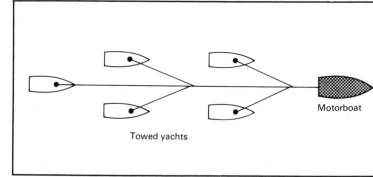

Towed yachts

Motorboat

authorities: in Britain, for instance, it is the Royal Yachting Association, based in London.

The IYRU is an organization composed of all the national federations. It has a Permanent Committee, and eleven other Committees, for: Keel Boats, Small Boats, International Regulations, Class Policy and Organization, Multihulls, Constitution, Youth Sailing, Racing Rules, Centreboard Boats, General Technical Matters; and a Committee on policy discussion. All boats of an international class recognized by the IYRU must, when they race abroad, have letters on their sails which indicate their nationality.

The International classes recognized by the IYRU are as follows:– The Finn; 505; Fireball; Flying Dutchman; Flying Junior; Cadet; Snipe; 420; 470; Vaurien; the International 14-foot; Star; Tempest; Tornado; Lightning; Australis; 'C' Class Cat; Contender; Enterprise; Moth; Optimist; Soling.

The Olympic Classes

Six classes will take part in the 1976 Olympic games. They will be the Flying Dutchman, Finn, Soling, Tempest, 470 and Tornado.

The Flying Dutchman
This is a centreboard boat for two crew, designed in 1951 by Dutchman Uilke van Essen. The boat has enjoyed great success thanks to the speed of the boat and the acrobatics needed to get the best of her, especially in a strong wind and flat sea. It was chosen as the Olympic class in Naples in 1960, and it still is 'Olympic'. It is a boat which needs most careful tuning and preparation; it needs a crew who are in harmony with each other and who are extremely fit.

Finn
The Finn is a one-design dinghy for singlehanded sailing, with a mast which has no shrouds, designed in 1952 by Richard Sarby for the Helsinki Olympic Games. Before this, the class for the Olympics was a yawl-rigged boat designed by Helmut Stanch in 1936, and then the Firefly, which was designed in 1946 by Uffa Fox and raced at Torquay in 1948. The Finn is best with a helmsman weighing at least 170 lbs (so that he will be at no disadvantage in a fresh breeze) and in good physical shape. In such a racing boat, the combined skill, muscle power, and technical knowledge of the man sailing the boat are of overriding importance.

Soling
The Soling was designed by Norwegian Jan Herman Linge as a one-design for the Olympics of 1972, where it took the place of the 5.5 metre; it has a crew of three and has a fine turn of speed. Its characteristics are: overall length 8.15 m (26.7 ft); waterline length 6.1 m (20 ft); beam 1.9 m (6.2 ft); draught 1.3 m (4.37 ft); displacement 1,000 kg (19.5 cwt); ballast 580 kg (11.25 cwt); sail area 21.7 m² (233 sq ft). It carries a spinnaker and is built in glassfibre.

Tempest
A one-design with bulb keel, this is the design of Englishman Ian Proctor, and like the Soling it took part in the 1972 Olympics for the first time. Main characteristics: overall length 6.7 m (22 ft); beam 1.97 m (6.5 ft); displacement 455 kg (8.75 cwt); weight of the bulb keel

227 kg (4.25 cwt); sail area 23 m² (247 sq ft). When racing it has a crew of two, and it is built in glassfibre.

Tornado
The question of whether a catamaran should be allowed into the Olympics is now decided, and the Tornado has been accepted for the next Games. In 1967 the IYRU held trials for A and B Class Catamarans. Rodney March designed for this event, Reg White advised on hull construction, and Terry Pearce on beams and spars. The simplicity of this design and an excellent performance produced the right boat. Main characteristics: overall length 6.1 m (19.9 ft); beam 3m (9.84 ft); displacement 135 kg (2.5 cwt); sail area 21.83 m² (234 sq ft).

470
The 470 has only recently been appointed to the Olympic ranks. It has a trapeze rig, and over 14,000 have been built since 1964, with the vast majority in France. André Cornu designed the boat, which is round-bilged, moulded in glassfibre. Main characteristics: overall length 4.7 m (15.4 ft); beam 1.7 m (5.6 ft); displacement 115 kg (2.25 cwt); sail area 26.52 m² (284 sq ft).

Catamarans

A catamaran has two hulls joined together with a bridge deck, and this type of craft has risen in popularity in recent years, both for racing and for cruising. The IYRU has encouraged the development of these boats as racing machines, and has given them three categories.
Category A: Singlehanded, with maximum beam of 2 m (6.6 ft) and about 14 m² of sail area (150 sq ft).
Category B: Two crewmen, a maximum beam of 3 m (9.8 ft), and a sail area of about 22 m² (236 sq ft).
Category C: Two crewmen, a maximum of 3.65 m (11.9 ft) of beam, and a sail area of about 28 m² (301 sq ft).

The sail area is calculated by taking the height to be that of the mast, and by allowing as much of the foot of the sail as you like.

The speed of a boat is worked out by calculating propulsive forces and the forces of resistance to its movement. The catamaran provides the opportunity of increasing the former and reducing the latter. It can, in fact, be steered when only one of its two hulls is in the water; the stability of a catamaran is great compared with its weight.

The sailing of a catamaran is slightly different from the sailing of a conventional boat because of its great speed, and so the apparent wind is brought forward and as a result the sails must be sheeted far further in. The mainsail is usually fully battened, with battens running right across the sail. The use of spinnakers on catamarans has not been very successful, especially in brisk winds, for the reasons mentioned above: the apparent wind comes too far forward. The Australians use spinnakers which are more like jibs, ballooned out and held by a pole.

Regattas

Competitions between sailing boats are called regattas. This name derives from a rowing race which was held on the Grand Canal in Venice, at the time of the Venetian Republic, and which is still held once every year, on

Corpus Christi Day. This name 'regatta' is used throughout the world.

Sailing boats which compete in regattas can be divided into two types:

1. One-design boats, which are built to a single plan; only the smallest of modifications are allowed within very precise limits.

2. Restricted classes. These can be built in different shapes, but the relationship between their main dimensions is defined in the class rules. For example, the rules of the 5.5 metre class as laid down by the IYRU are as follows:

$$R = 0.9 \frac{L\sqrt{S}}{12\sqrt[3]{D}} + \frac{L + \sqrt{S}}{4} \le 5.5$$

R (Rating): a linear unit.

L (Length): the length, that is above the waterline, with corrections dependent on the shape of the boat.

S (Sail area): the real surface of the sails, measured in square metres.

D (Displacement): displacement in cubic metres (1,025.21 kg per square metre).

$\sqrt{}$ S: square root of the sail in square metres.

$\sqrt{}$ D: square root of the displacement in cubic metres.

The course of a race in a regatta may be triangular or a straight line (there and back). It is marked out by buoys, or beacons, or various other shapes, which may or may not carry flags on them. There are other types of course, but all are based on triangular or straight line courses, and often combine the two – for example, an Olympic course for the Star Class, shown in the diagram. (The Star will not be classed in the next Olympic Games.)

In general, the regatta racing committee will moor the racing buoys at the very last moment and in such a way that, given the direction of the wind, the first leg of the course will be made to windward. There are also race courses fixed by clubs well in advance of the race, between permanently moored buoys. The committee may then alter the angle of the starting line, depending on the direction of the wind.

On the Swiss lakes, where the winds are very variable, a course is given, and it can be modified by signals which can be seen by the competitors as they pass by the committee after the first round of the course. In races with three rounds, the course can still be changed after the second round.

Points

There are many different systems for deciding who is the winner when there is a series of races.

The simplest system

The simplest system is worked out as follows: one point to the first yacht to finish, two to the second, three to the third, and so on. A competitor who does not start, who abandons the race or is disqualified, receives as many points as boats entered in the race.

The Olympic system

There are seven races in all, and of these, six will count towards the prize. For each race, the first boat gets zero points, the second 3 points, and third 5.7 points, the fourth 8 points, the fifth 10 points, the sixth 11.7 points, and from the seventh, you add on 6 points to your place. Thus if you should come eighth you get 8 + 6 = 14 points, and so on. A boat abandoning the race during the course of that race gets the same number of points as the last to arrive. A boat not starting gets the same number of points as the number of boats entered for the contest. A boat

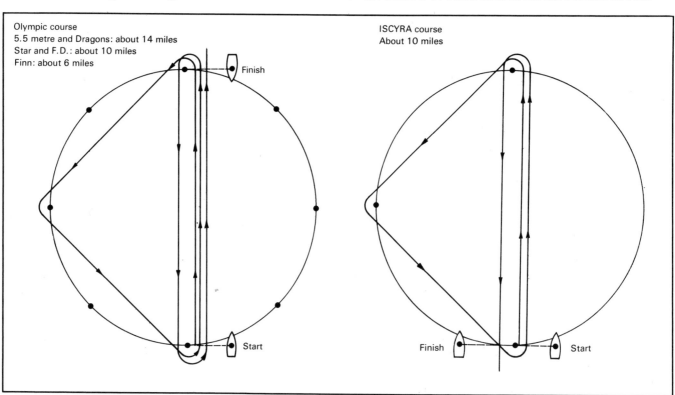

Olympic course
5.5 metre and Dragons: about 14 miles
Star and F.D.: about 10 miles
Finn: about 6 miles

Finish

Start

ISCYRA course
About 10 miles

Finish

Start

which is disqualified gets the same number of points as the last boat to arrive, increased by 10 points per 100 boats taking part (rounded up to the nearest whole number). The boat which has managed to achieve the lowest number of points after all the races are over is nominated the winner.

Example in a regatta of three races: 49 entered.
1st race – 39 starters.

A boat abandoning the race gets	45 points = 39 + 6
A boat not starting gets	49 points
A boat disqualified gets	49 points = 39 + 10

2nd race – 43 starters.

A boat abandoning the race gets	49 points = 43 +,6
A boat not starting gets	49 points
A boat disqualified gets	53 points = 43 + 10

3rd race – 40 starters.

A boat abandoning the race gets	46 points = 40 + 6
A boat not starting gets	49 points
A boat disqualified gets	50 points = 40 + 10

International Star Class Yacht Racing Association System
This is based on the average of placings obtained in the course of five races, and it is worked out as follows:

One point for each course finished, and one for each boat beaten. A boat which does not start, abandons the race, or is disqualified, gets zero points. When boats finish with a tie, you add up the total of points which they would have received if they had finished separately, and then divide the points between the tied boats.

The SCIRA systems
The SCIRA Class (Snipe Class International Racing Association) is also based on an average of points and is calculated thus:

The number of points given is worked out from the number of boats that finish the race, and then according to their order of arrival. If two or more competitors pass the finishing post at the same moment, they each get the number of points corresponding to their place, and following boats receive their points as if the tied boats had arrived separately. The table of points for a fleet of 40 boats reads, for instance, as follows: 1,600 points to the first, 1,521 points to the second, 1,444 points to the third, 1,369 points to the fourth . . . and 1 point to the fortieth.

Formula of the IOR

The International Offshore Rule is a formula for handicapping offshore racing boats, to allow boats of many different sizes to race together. Previously two major rules dominated the world, those of the Royal Ocean Racing Club and of the Cruising Club of America: now the new IOR rule holds good throughout the vast majority of the world's big boat racers.

$$\text{MR (measured rating)} = 0.15\frac{L\sqrt{S}}{\sqrt{BD}} + 0.20(L + \sqrt{S}) + DC + FC$$

The figures for the rating must be calculated to four figures of decimals in metres.
Rating R = MR × EPF × CGF
Where L = rated length, to the nearest fourth place in metres.
S = The calculated sail area in square metres to two places of decimals.
B = Rated beam in metres to the nearest fourth place of decimals.

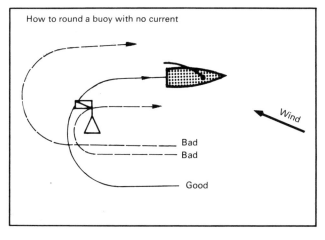

How to round a buoy with no current

Wind
Bad
Bad
Good

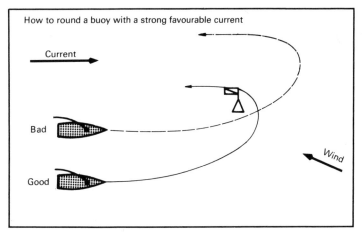

How to round a buoy with a strong favourable current

Current
Bad
Good
Wind

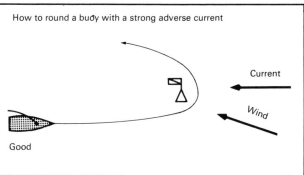

How to round a buoy with a strong adverse current

Current
Wind
Good

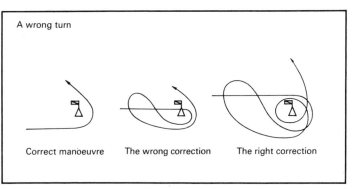

A wrong turn

Correct manoeuvre   The wrong correction   The right correction

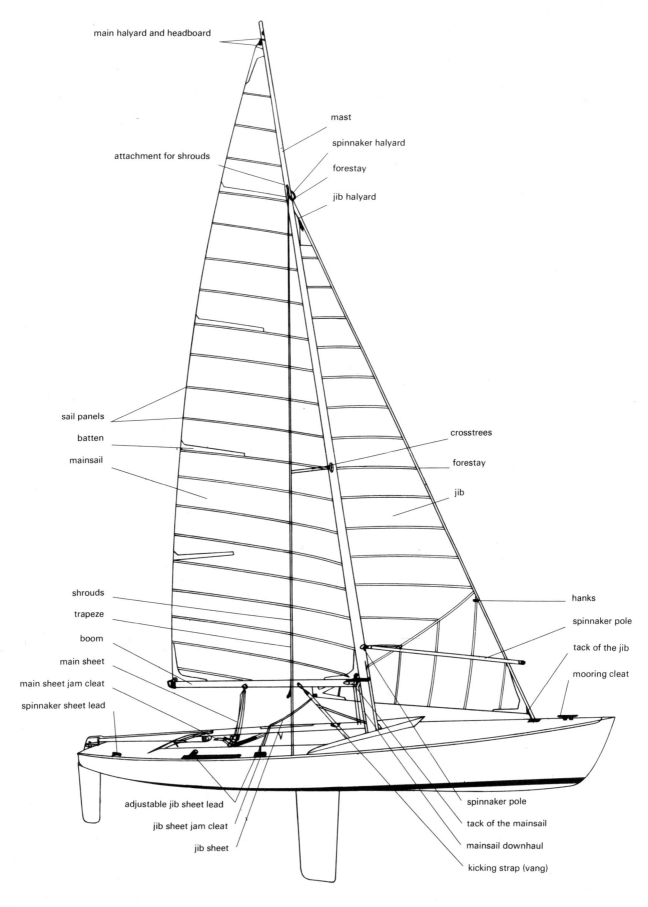

main halyard and headboard

mast

spinnaker halyard

forestay

jib halyard

attachment for shrouds

sail panels

batten

mainsail

crosstrees

forestay

jib

shrouds

trapeze

boom

main sheet

main sheet jam cleat

spinnaker sheet lead

hanks

spinnaker pole

tack of the jib

mooring cleat

adjustable jib sheet lead

jib sheet jam cleat

jib sheet

spinnaker pole

tack of the mainsail

mainsail downhaul

kicking strap (vang)

D = Depth in metres to the nearest fourth place of decimals.
DC = A draft correction to the nearest fourth place.
FC = A freeboard correction to the nearest fourth place.
EPF = A factor for the engine and the propeller, to the nearest fourth decimal place.
CGF = The centre of gravity factor, to the nearest fourth decimal place.

When a yacht has got her rating (in feet), she will then race in the following classes (or in whatever classes are decided locally).

Class I:	From 33 to 70 feet
Class II:	From 29 to 33 feet
Class III:	From 25.5 to 29 feet
Class IV:	From 23 to 25.5 feet
Class V:	From 21 to 23 feet
Class VI:	From 16 to 21 feet

Racing tactics

To round a buoy when there is no current, the boat follows round the arc of a circle. The manoeuvre will be quicker when the buoy is at the top of the arc.

To round the buoy with a strong following current: If you head straight for the buoy, then you cannot properly describe the arc of a circle; the current will take you far away from the buoy, and you will go a longer distance. So you must head away from the buoy and round it close by.

To round a buoy with a strong foul current, you must approach the buoy and go round it as close as you can, to make the best use of the current which will be following you after you have rounded the buoy.

If you make an error and leave the buoy on the wrong side, for instance by leaving on your right a buoy which you should have left on your left, then you must undo the wrong you have done before you pass the buoy on the correct side: if a string were to be laid along your course, it must pull straight to pass the buoy on the correct side.

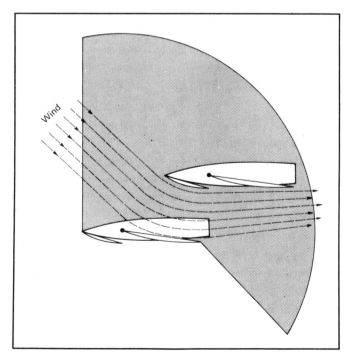

When two boats are competing at close quarters, on the same tack, the boat to leeward is in a better position than the windward boat, as long as it is at least half a boat's length ahead. What happens is that the wind deflected by the leeward boat's sails interferes with the wind pattern of the windward boat, and the leeward boat can also squeeze up to windward and ahead of the other boat, and really give her 'dirty' wind. This is why, when you are on port tack, coming up to a starboard hand tack boat (which has right of way) you should consider an alternative to bearing off to pass under your rival's stern. You could also tack to leeward, seeking to get into this 'safe leeward position'. You have to calculate this manoeuvre carefully so that you have enough speed on your new tack to get into the safe position, otherwise the windward boat will be able to get ahead of you and take all your wind from your sails.

The starting line is made by lining up a flag placed on a mast on the committee boat, and a flag on a buoy. The distance between these two starting marks is chosen by the committee boat after it has determined the number of boats entered in the race. If the start is from a sailing club, then the flag and mast may be on one side of the clubhouse, provided it can be easily seen from the sea. The buoy limiting the starting line may be moored facing the club, and at a convenient distance, again depending on the number of starters. After the start, the buoy can become a turning mark with competitors sailing round it to start a second round of the course.

The starting line becomes the finishing line at the end of the race, unless the rules of the course state otherwise, and the competitors will be told to pass through the line as each round of the race ends.

Ten minutes before the time for the start of the race, the committee hoists the flag of that race, and a flag which tells competitors the course to be followed. A gun fires at the same time as these flags are hoisted. Five minutes before the start, another gun is fired and the warning signal is hoisted (the flag P in the International Code of Signals). At this moment the rules of racing come into play, but the competitors still have to manoeuvre around without being able to start. Then the starting gun fires and the flags are lowered. If a yacht is over the starting line at the start, it has to face a recall gun, and return to the right side of the line to start again.

Racing rules

Racing rules can be found in the international edicts of the IYRU: they aim primarily to avoid collisions during the course of the race. Here are some important items from the Racing Rules:

Article 36. Yachts on opposite tacks: a port-tack yacht shall keep clear of a starboard-tack yacht.

Article 37. Yachts on the same point of sailing:
1. A windward yacht shall keep clear of a leeward yacht.
2. A yacht clear astern shall keep clear of a yacht clear ahead.
3. A yacht which established an overlap to leeward from clear astern shall allow the windward yacht ample room and opportunity to keep clear, and during the existence of that overlap the leeward yacht shall not sail above her proper course.

Bibliography

Baader, Juan *The Sailing Yacht* Adlard Coles, London
   1962; Norton, New York 1965.

Boyd, Patrick *Catamarans in Close Up* Ian Allan, London
   1972.

Brown, Alan *Invitation to Sailing* Adlard Coles, London
   1962; Simon & Schuster, New York 1968.

Bruce, Erroll *Deep Sea Sailing* Stanley Paul, London 1953;
   De Graff, New York, Revised Edn. 1967.

Chapelle, H.I. *Yacht Designing and Planning* Norton,
   New York 1936; Allen & Unwin, London 1972.

Elvstrom, Paul *Yacht Racing* Nautical Publishing,
   Hampshire 1970.

Fletcher, M. and Ross, R. *Tuning a Racing Yacht*
   Angus & Robertson, London 1972.

Grell, Gunther *Beginners Book of Sailing* Ward Lock,
   London 1968.

Oakeley, J.D.A. *Winning* Nautical Publishing, Hampshire
   1970.

Twimane, Eric *Dinghy Team Racing* Granada Publishing,
   London 1971.

Walker, Stuart *The Tactics of Small Boat Racing*
   Hodder & Stoughton, London 1966; Norton,
   New York 1966.

1 A typical cruising yawl on a broad reach with plenty of canvas set provides a good example of spars, sails and rigging, as detailed in the diagram.

1	Mainsail	13	Shroud
2	Mizzen	14	Lowers
3	Spinnaker stays'l	15	Forestay
4	Spinnaker	16	Backstay, running rigging
5	Mizzen stays'l, spars	17	Topping lift
6	Main mast	18	Main sheet
7	Mizzen mast	19	Spinnaker sheet
8	Main boom	20	Spinnaker pole downhaul
9	Mizzen boom	21	Spinnaker pole topping lift
10	Spinnaker pole	22	Jib sheet
11	Crosstrees	23	Spinnaker halyard
12	Battens, standing rigging		

2

3

2 An Egyptian sailing boat. Queen Cleopatra was the first person to have a sailing boat purely for pleasure.

3 A caravel, the ship of the great navigators who discovered new continents and new civilizations for Europe.

4 An old-fashioned three-masted schooner. This is *Palinuro,* a sail training ship of the Italian Navy. Dimensions: overall length 68.9 m (77.4 ft); beam 10.1 m (33.1 ft); weight 1341 tonnes (1321 tons); draught 4.9 m (13.42 ft); sail area 898 m² (1074 sq ft); 375 hp engine.

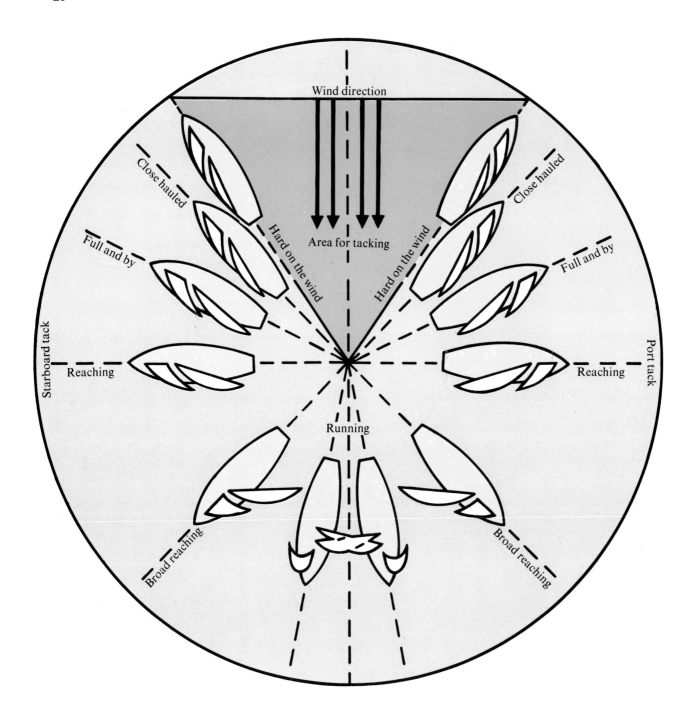

Wind direction

Area for tacking

Close hauled

Close hauled

Full and by

Full and by

Hard on the wind

Hard on the wind

Starboard tack

Port tack

Reaching

Reaching

Running

Broad reaching

Broad reaching

5 5.5 metres, hard on the wind, most of them on starboard tack, after the start of the International regatta at Genoa in 1968.

6

6 Stars on a reach, off Trieste. On this point of sailing the Star, in spite of its weight, manages to start planing in winds over 20 knots.

7 On the run, during the International regatta at Genoa in 1968, are two world champions, Commandant Straulino from Italy in *Manuela VII*, and the Swiss Noverraz in *Toucan VIII*.

8 The Class I ocean racer *Deneb*, on a broad reach with all sails set – from the front: spinnaker, spinnaker stays'l, mainsail, mizzen stays'l, and mizzen.

7 8

10

9 Soling This one-design three man keelboat replaced the 5.5 metre in the 1972 Olympics. It is designed by Norway's Jan Herman Linge. Dimensions: overall length 8.15 m (26.7 ft); waterline length 6.1 m (20 ft); beam 1.9 m (6.2 ft); draught 1.3 m (4.27 ft); weight 1,000 kg (19.5 cwt); sail area 21.7 m² (233 sq ft); built in glassfibre.

10 Tornado Not so long ago the Olympics were dominated by keel boats, a breed fast vanishing. Now the Olympic Games have come to represent more nearly the type of boat sailed throughout the world, with emphasis on dinghies – and at last a catamaran, the Tornado, is allowed into the Games. We look forward to seeing how this catamaran fares, and whether the Olympics will expand further and include an ocean racer by 1980. Dimensions: overall length 6.09 m (19.9 ft); waterline length 5.78 m (18.9 ft); beam 3 m (9.84 ft); draught 0.15–0.75 m (0.5–2.46 ft); displacement 135 kg (2.5 cwt); sail area 21.83 m² (234 sq ft).

11

11 470 Now an Olympic class. It has a glassfibre hull built within small tolerances: its buoyant forward section gives it good performance in high waves; it has a trapeze rig. Three independent watertight compartments make it self-rescuing. Over 14,000 were sold in more than thirty countries, even before the class was given Olympic status. Dimensions: overall length 4.7 m (15.6 ft); waterline length 4.44 m (14.5 ft); beam 1.7 m (5.6 ft); draught 1 m (3.3 ft); weight in sailing trim 115 kg (2.25 cwt); sail area 13.3 m² (142 sq ft).

12

12 Flying Dutchman A one-design dinghy designed in 1951 by Dutchman Uilke van Essen. Dimensions: overall length 6.05 m (19.8 ft); beam 1.7 m (5.6 ft); weight 160 kg (3 cwt); sail area 18 m² (193 sq ft); racing crew – two; built in wood or glassfibre. The photograph shows a boat from the Federal German Republic (the letter G).

13   Finn   A one-design dinghy for singlehanded racing, designed in 1952 by Richard Sarby for the Helsinki Olympic Games. Dimensions: overall length 4.5 m (14.7 ft); beam 1.51 m (4.95 ft); weight 145 kg (2.75 cwt); sail area 10 m² (107 sq ft); built in wood or glassfibre. Here is a French competitor (the letter F).

14

14 **Tempest** A one-design with a bulb keel designed by England's Ian Proctor, participating in the Olympics for the first time in 1972. Dimensions: overall length 6.7 m (22 ft); beam 1.97 m (6.5 ft); weight 455 kg (8.75 cwt); weight of the bulb keel 227 kg (4.25 cwt); sail area 23 m² (247 sq ft); racing crew – two; built in fibreglass.

15

16

17

15   12 foot dinghy   A one-design created in 1913 by G. Gockspott, and still a popular class. It is unusual these days in that it has a gunter rig. Dimensions: overall length 3.66 m (12 ft); beam 1.42 m (4.66 ft); draught 0.48 m (1.57 ft); weight 115 kg (2.25 cwt); sail area 9.3 m² (99 sq ft); built in wood.

16   Moth   Here is the American version of the Moth. In Europe there are other types of Moth, English and French, which are very popular (their sail insignia is an 'M'). Dimensions: overall length 3.55 m (11.65 ft); beam 1.44 m (4.72 ft); weight 60 kg (1 cwt); sail area 7 m² (75 sq ft); built in wood or glassfibre.

17   O K dinghy   This one-design was created by the Dane, Knud Olsen with the idea of introducing young people to singlehanded racing on a less expensive boat than the Finn. Dimensions: overall length 4 m (13.12 ft); beam 1.42 m (4.66 ft); weight 72 kg (1.25 cwt); sail area 8.30 m² (89 sq ft); built in glassfibre.

18 Cadet A one-design dinghy intended for international competition between young people. Dimensions: overall length 3.22 m (10.56 ft); beam 1.27 m (4.17 ft); weight 75 kg (1.3 cwt); sail area 5.65 m² (59.5 sq ft); racing crew – two; built in wood.

19 Zef A one-design dinghy for two, both for learning and for racing. Dimensions: overall length 3.67 m (12.04 ft); beam 1.55 m (5.09 ft); weight 90 kg (1.75 cwt); sail area 8.5 m² (91 sq ft); built in wood or glassfibre. Can be sailed singlehanded.

18

19

20

21

20　Vaurien　One-design dinghy made in 1953 by Herbulot, one of the most prolific of French designers. Because of its low price this class has great popularity. Today there are over 20,000 of them, of which 12,000 are in France. Dimensions: overall length 4.08 m (13.39 ft); beam 1.47 m (4.82 ft); weight 95 kg (1.75 cwt); sail area 8.8 m² (94 sq ft); racing crew – two; built in glassfibre.

21　Flying Junior　One-design dinghy, created by Uilke van Essen in 1955. Used for teaching sailing because of its easy handling and manoeuvrability. It allows the young to prepare for the Flying Dutchman, a more sophisticated type of boat. Dimensions: overall length 4.03 m (3.22 ft); beam 1.5 m (4.92 ft); weight 90 kg (1.8 cwt); sail area 9.3 m² (99 sq ft); racing crew – two; built in glassfibre and wood.

22　Snipe　One-design dinghy designed in 1931 by William Crosby. Acknowledged as an International Class, it can be found throughout the world. Its owners are grouped in national fleets, and the headquarters of the Class Association are in the United States, where the design was conceived. Dimensions: overall length 4.72 m (15.5 ft); beam 1.52 m (5 ft); weight 198 kg (3.8 cwt); sail area 10.7 m² (114 sq ft); racing crew – two; built in glassfibre or wood.

23　420　A one-design centreboard dinghy created in 1960 by Christian Maury, which has had considerable success. Dimensions: overall length 4.2 m (13.8 ft); beam 1.63 m (5.35 ft); weight 98 kg (1.27 cwt); sail area 10.25 m² (109.5 sq ft); racing crew – two; built in glassfibre or wood.

22

23

24 Sharpie A lively one-design centreboarder designed by H. Kroger in 1927. It had its hour of glory when it was selected for the Olympic games in Melbourne in 1956. Dimensions: overall length 5.99 m (19.7 ft); beam 1.43 m (4.7 ft); weight 280 kg (5.5 cwt) sail area 16.2 m² (174 sq ft); built in wood. Here is *Romolo,* fourth at Melbourne, crewed by Capio and Massino.

25 505 A one-design dinghy, by John Westall. It was made in 1953 and christened Coronet in tribute to the coronation of Queen Elizabeth II of England. It has never received the accolade that it deserves, for the Flying Dutchman was chosen in its place for the Olympics. In 1961 the IYRU recognized its status by classifying it as a Class A International one-design. Dimensions: overall length 5.028 m (16.5 ft); beam 1.865 m (6.1 ft); sail area 16.21 m² (172 sq ft); racing crew – two; built in glassfibre or wood.

24

25

26   The Dane Paul Elvstrom can, perhaps, be called the reigning world champion of sail. After winning four gold medals for singlehanded sailing at the Olympics in 1948, 1952, 1956 and 1960, he has collected world championships in a wide variety of craft – Snipe, Flying Dutchman, 5.5 metres – and he won the World Championship in 1966 in the Star *Scandale* (his crew was John Albrechtson), at Kiel. In 1967 he won it again, in the same boat but with a different crew, at Copenhagen. In this photograph Elvstrom is sailing along after a race.

27   **Merope** is a famous name among the Italian racing fraternity. Among its more brilliant victories were a gold and then a silver medal at the Olympics at Helsinki and Melbourne, three world championships, and nine European championships. Here is *Merope III* at Melbourne.

28   The Star *Taifun* of the Russians Pineguine and Shutkov rounding a buoy during the International regatta at Genoa in 1968. This crew won the gold medal with the Star *Tornado* at Naples in 1960 (the Rome Olympics), and won the European Championship in 1964.

29   England's Pattison and MacDonald at Genoa in 1968, where they won two races. They then dominated the Flying Dutchman class at Sanremo with the best helmsmen in the world taking part, to become world champions. They won an Olympic gold medal at Acapulco, and another at Kiel in 1972.

30   **Lightning** A one-design with a very brisk performance, conceived in 1939 by Olin Stephens, one of the most remarkable of America's yacht designers. It is suitable for cruising around, and is also fast in races with a spinnaker of sizeable proportions. It has not had the success it deserves, perhaps because of a certain lack of elegance. Dimensions: overall length 5.79 m (19 ft); beam 1.987 m (3.22 ft); weight 317.5 kg (6.2 cwt); sail area 16.3 m² (175 sq ft); racing crew – three; built in glassfibre or wood. Here is *Kalimero*, European champion in 1965, crewed by Tulli, Fagnano and Palomba.

32

31 Red Rooster This is a design by Dick Carter of America. It is a
compromise between an ocean racer and a dinghy; its keel swivels upwards and
its rudder can be raised just as in a dinghy, but it has a crew and sails the
courses of the offshore fleet. An innovator, Dick designed that giant over
100 ft long, *Vendredi Treize,* for the last Observer Singlehanded Race. Red
Rooster's statistics are: overall length 12.4 m (40.6 ft); waterline length 9.6 m
(31.5 ft); beam 3.7 m (12.14 ft); draught (centreboard lowered) 8.8 m (28.8 ft).

32 Under the command of the well known helmsman Eric Tabarly, who had
much success in singlehanded racing and in fully-crewed ocean racing, *Pen
Duick III* a Class II RORC yacht, won the classic Fastnet race in 1967. It has a
bulbous keel, but the rudder is separate from it and is almost at the end of
the hull. Dimensions: overall length 17.45 (56.5 ft); waterline length 13 m
(14.2 ft); draught 4.2 m (13.8 ft); sail area 148 m² (1,593 sq ft); weight
13,400 kg (13.2 tons); ballast 6,310 kg (6 tons); 10 berths.

33   The Italian *Alnair IV*, designed by Stephens, belongs to the Class III
RORC, but it is also listed among One Ton Cup boats designed for regatta
sailing, a class which one would like to see admitted to the Olympic Games.
Dimensions: overall length 11.2 m (36.2 ft); waterline length 8.4 m (27.56 ft);
beam 3.09 m (10.14 ft); displacement 7 tonnes (6.85 tons); draught 1.96 m
(6.43 ft); sail area 50 m² (538 sq ft).

34   *Arpège* is a Class V RORC racer of French build, which has been very
successful because of its speed, ease of handling and good accommodation.
Dimensions: overall length 9 m (29.5 ft); waterline length 6.7 m (22 ft); beam
3 m (9.8 ft); draught 1.35 m (4.4 ft); sail area 37 m² (44.25 sq ft); weight
3,000 kg (2.9 tons); ballast 1,200 kg (20.5 cwt); six berths.

35 Ecume de Mer One of the small cruiser-racers built in France which are cheap, fast and attractive. With 5-6 berths, standing headroom and easy handling, it makes an ideal boat, and won the Quarter Ton Cup in 1970. Ecume's dimensions are: overall length 7.93 m (26 ft); waterline length 5.87 m (19.25 ft); beam 2.71 m (8.9 ft); draught 1.25 m (4.1 ft) cruising, and 1.53 m (5 ft) racing.

36

36 Golif   A small offshore keelboat, seaworthy and good in difficult sea
conditions, which has been most popular. Dimensions: overall length 6.5 m
(21.3 ft); beam 2.26 m (7.4 ft); draught 1.13 m (4.3 ft); sail area 20.1 m²
(216 sq ft); weight 1,250 kg (20.6 cwt); four berths, built in glassfibre.

37

38

39

40

37 Requin Created in France in 1934 as a one-design racing cruiser. It is a sea-going yacht despite its weight and has been very popular both for racing and for cruising. Dimensions: overall length 9.6 m (31.5 ft); beam 1.9 m (6.23 ft); draught 1.1 m (3.6 ft); weight 1,780 kg (35.25 cwt); sail area 25 m² (29.9 sq ft); three berths; racing crew – three; built in wood.

38 Regent Keelboat of medium size, dreamed up by the firm who built the Golif, partly from their experience with the latter boat. Dimensions: overall length 8.36 m (27.4 ft); beam 2.49 m (8.17 ft); draught 1.3 m (4.3 ft); sail area 33 m² (355 sq ft); weight 3,000 kg (2.95 tons); ballast 1,020 kg (20 cwt); five berths; built in glassfibre. Other boats of the same type – Victorian, Attila, Wibo IV, Super Chenal, Spartacus, Estuaire 18.

39 Alpa 9 A smallish cruiser built by Alpa, whose boats have been much in demand from an international clientèle. It is a very seaworthy keelboat. Dimensions: overall length 9.09 m (29.8 ft); beam 2.7 m (8.8 ft); draught 1.6 m (5.25 ft); weight 3,900 kg (3.8 tons); sail area 32.4 m² (38.6 sq ft); four or five berths; built in glassfibre.

40 Hurley 22 Built in England, practical and safe in all weather conditions. It is convenient for short and medium length passages, as it is carefully balanced. Dimensions: overall length 6.7 m (21.9 ft); beam 2.22 m (7.28 ft); draught 1.14 m (3.7 ft); weight 1,768 kg (34.5 cwt); ballast 1,043 kg (20.25 cwt); sail area 22.32 m² (239 sq ft); four berths; built in glassfibre.

The Classic Ocean Races

A Bermuda From Newport (Rhode Island) to Bermuda. Distance 630 miles. Run every two years, in June. The greater part of the race is usually sailed on a broad reach. After yachts cross the sweep of the Gulf Stream, the winds are usually light (though in 1972 they were unusually severe).

B California-Honolulu The start is usually from San Pedro. Distance 2,500 miles. This is the longest of established races in the world, apart from the transoceanic races which can be set over 3,000 miles and more. Usually the winds blow from astern, which frequently causes damage to halyards and spinnakers.

C The Fastnet About 650 miles This contest is held every two years, leaving from Cowes in the Isle of Wight. After sailing along the south-west coastline of England and across the sea to Ireland, the competitors round the Fastnet Rock and come back to Plymouth to finish. The course is difficult and interesting because of the variable tides, variable weather (sometimes extremely heavy), and the proximity of rocky and dangerous shores. The photograph (**41**) shows *Pen Duick III*, winner of the 1967 Fastnet, near *Levantades*, a Class I racer, which came sixth in the event.

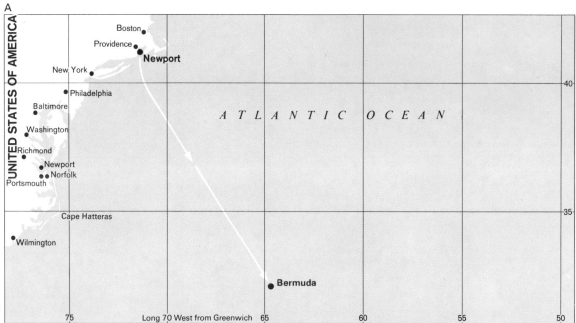

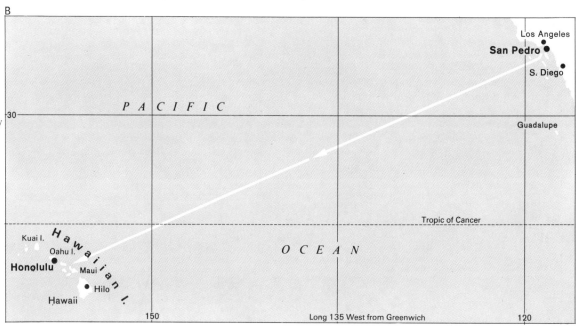

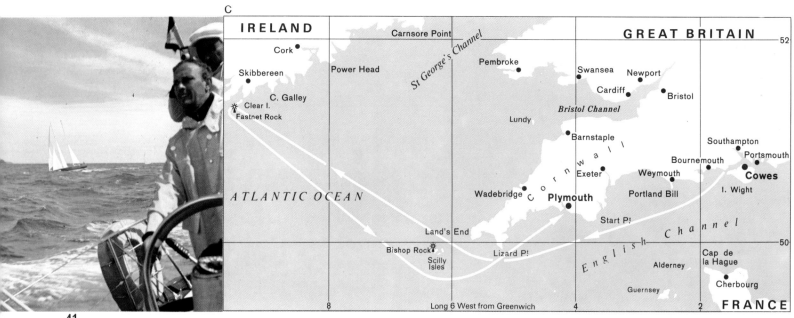

D   Buenos Aires-Rio de Janeiro   Distance 1,200 miles. A race held every three years. The start is from the River Plate. After navigating along the coastline of Uruguay and Brazil, the competitors arrive in the bay of Rio de Janeiro. On the race the winds are variable and sometimes very stormy.

E   Sydney-Hobart   650 miles. Held every year, the start is from the magnificent harbour of Sydney. After sailing along the New South Wales coastline and crossing the Bass Straight, yachts sail along the Tasmanian coastline to finish at Hobart, Tasmania's capital. The race is held at the end of December, during the Australian summer. Winds are variable, with sudden alterations of direction.

F   The Giraglia   About 240 miles. The start changes each year, alternating between Sanremo, Toulon and Saint-Tropez. After rounding the island of Giraglia, at the extreme north of Corsica, the fleet reaches either the Italian port or one of the two French ports. The winds are very variable, both in strength and direction, with long calms giving way to violent blows. Plate **42** shows the start of a Giraglia Race from Sanremo.

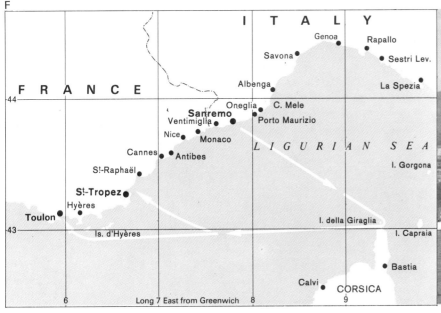

The fabulous 12 metres
The competition which carries most prestige in front of the world's audience
is the Americas Cup. It has been fought for since 1851. The holders are
American, and the cup has been won by the United States in every contest to
date: the representatives of any other nation which beat the holders would
make the history books. Before the Second World War the race was contested
in J Class yachts, with a length of 30 metres and masts 50 metres high. Since
1958 the contest has been rather in 12 metres, which are far less costly.
Usually the building of a 12 metre is by a syndicate of people excited by the
sport of sailing. They gather round them the best sailmakers, designers,
builders and crews that they can muster. Here are the holders and
challengers in 12 metres:
1958 *Columbia* (USA) beat *Sceptre* (England)
1962 *Weatherly* (USA) beat *Gretel* (Australia)
1964 *Constellation* (USA) beat *Sovereign* (England)
1967 *Intrepid* (USA) beat *Dame Pattie* (Australia)
1970 *Intrepid* (USA) beat *Gretel II* (Australia)

43, 44 Australia's *Gretel II* challenges *Intrepid* (USA) for the 1970 Americas
Cup.

45 Australia's *Dame Pattie* on a broad reach, on port tack.

46 England's *Sovereign*, designed by David Boyd, close hauled on starboard
tack.

47 Offshore multihulls have developed fast over the last decades. Trimarans (three hulled) have done extremely well; catamarans (two hulled) also cross oceans. Here is a cat designed by Rudi Choy and owned by Australia's Bill Howell. Named *Golden Cockerel* and later *Tahiti Bill*, it has made singlehanded transatlantic crossings.

48 Hobie 14 The Hobie catamaran has enjoyed a fast rise in popularity, and more than 2,000 skippers sail them regularly in regattas. They are also most popular with the young and with those who sail from beaches, as they can be easily launched and recovered from places where dinghies and keelboats would find it difficult. Dimensions: overall length 4.27 m (14.01 ft); beam 2.34 m (7.68 ft); displacement 100 kg (1.75 cwt); sail area 11 m² (118 sq ft).

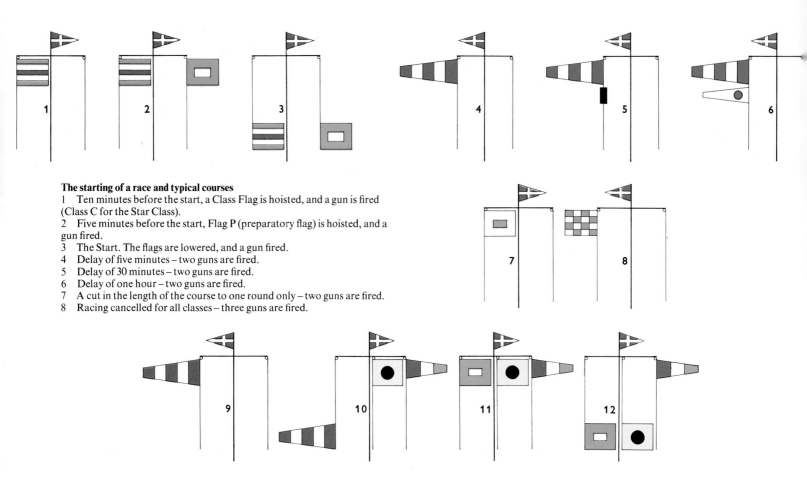

The starting of a race and typical courses

1 Ten minutes before the start, a Class Flag is hoisted, and a gun is fired (Class C for the Star Class).

2 Five minutes before the start, Flag P (preparatory flag) is hoisted, and a gun fired.

3 The Start. The flags are lowered, and a gun fired.

4 Delay of five minutes – two guns are fired.

5 Delay of 30 minutes – two guns are fired.

6 Delay of one hour – two guns are fired.

7 A cut in the length of the course to one round only – two guns are fired.

8 Racing cancelled for all classes – three guns are fired.

An example of starting signals: supposing that the 5.5 metres starts at 11 o'clock, and the jury decides to postpone the start for 15 minutes and hoists the signal for delay (the ring pennant). At the end of the 15 minutes the jury decides on course 3 and hoists flag number 3. In this case the signal would appear as follows:

9 At 10.50, the answering pennant is hoisted – two guns fired.

10 At 11.05, the answering pennant is lowered and flag number 3 raised – flag I (the class flag) is hoisted – one gun fired.

11 At 11.10, the preparatory flag P is hoisted – one gun fired.

12 At 11.15, the start – flags I and P lowered – one gun fired.

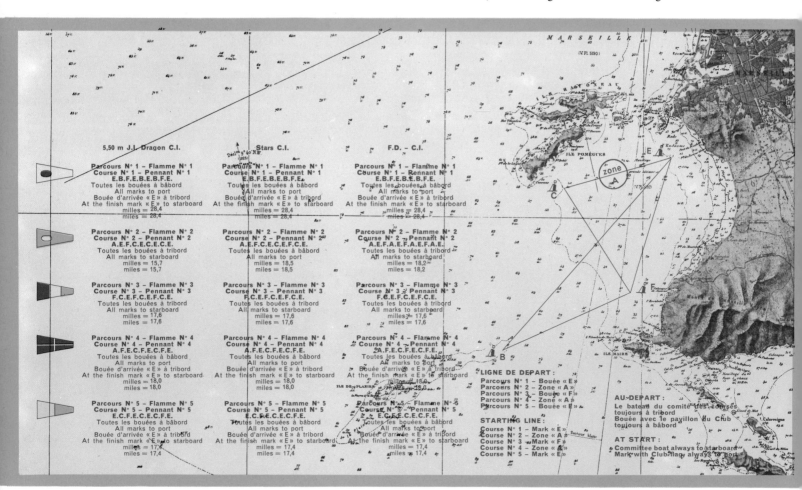

49 **50**

51

Racing Rules and Tactics

Make a good start and you are well on the way to victory. But while it is difficult for competitors to make a good start, it is equally hard for the race organizers to make a good starting line.

49–52   Here (**49**) is a good starting line which does not much favour any of the competitors starting on the wind. The following photographs (**50, 51, 52**) show that a position near to the Committee Boat has given an advantage since, less than a minute from the start, the boats up to windward are indeed in the lead.

52

53 Article 37 (1) of the racing rules. 'A windward yacht shall keep clear of a leeward yacht'. Here Finn 358, on the same tack and closing, must leave room for Finn 253.

54 Article 36 (1), a fundamental rule. 'A port tack yacht shall keep clear of a starboard tack yacht'. Star 1-5087 must give way to the other boats.

55 Definitions: the 5.5 metre I-54 is 'clear ahead' of the 5.5 metre Z-70. This latter is 'clear astern' of the former. I-52 is to windward of Z-70.

56 After rounding a buoy, it is a good rule to luff up gently, as has the Star M-5071, so as not to have your wind taken and so to remain ahead of the other boats.

57

57 The boat X-5084, which has to tack to leave the buoy to port (on her left hand side), must watch the boats arriving on starboard tack, giving them room (articles 36 and 41 of the rules).

58 All three starboard tack boats are about to round the mark, which they must leave to port. The yacht in third place has no right, if he has no overlap on the second boat within two lengths of the buoy, to pass to leeward, between that second boat and the buoy.

59 The two boats 5145 and 5148, which are close hauled on the starboard

58

tack, have the right of way over all the others, which have just rounded the buoy and are coming back with the wind astern. When making a course after rounding a buoy be careful to avoid colliding with nearby boats.

60 Approaching the buoy in the manner shown by the leading boat, which is heading very close to the wind (pinching), lowers the speed and is very dangerous, for the other boats, which have been on that tack for a long time and have greater speed, can take the leading boat's wind (blanket the boat). A slight unfavourable current is sufficient to drive the boat onto the buoy, which may lead to disqualification.

60

61 After making a tack, it is not necessary to bring in the jib before establishing the fact that you are on a new tack. It is necessary to place the crew's weight to windward, first to sail with the jib slightly free so that the boat can pick up speed, and then to haul in the sheet.

62 After rounding the buoy it is necessary, if you are leading, to escape being 'blanketed' (having the wind taken from your sails) by the boats which are following you, on their new point of sailing with the wind behind them. If you are slowed down by 'blanketing' try to choose a different course from the boats directly behind you, in the hope of getting a clear wind.

63–64 The astute skipper who is off the wind tries to 'blanket' the yacht in front, and the manoeuvre which is made to try and avoid this is called a 'luffing match'. Here is a struggle of this type between two famous yachts, *Artica II* and *Alnair IV*.

65 The approach to a buoy by a number of yachts at speed demands, on the part of competitors, prompt reflexes and cool determination.

63 64

65

66–68 To get more speed than the other yachts you must start at full pace. Observe the start of the 5.5 metres during the International regatta at Genoa in 1968. Z-88 starts in the middle of the line, with clear wind from its rivals, and freed off the wind slightly. 1-52 (plate **67**) cannot pass it, as it cannot come closer to the wind and its speed is disturbed by wind backeddies from Z-88. In the following pictures 1-52 has lost ground, while 1-42 (in a better position than Z-70) and Z-88 have increased their advantage. Z-88 will be the winner of this race.

69–70 Arriving at the buoy on a run, the 5.5 metre 1-49 comes onto the wind. As the boat is 100 m ahead of the second boat, after 50 m from the buoy it becomes necessary, tactically, to tack again onto port tack, so that he can then be right upwind of the rival yacht when it reaches the buoy. In that way he can then match every move his rival makes.

3

4

71 Going from a reach to wind dead astern, the competitors fan out to avoid their sails being masked by others astern. If the wind is steady, it is necessary to take the most direct route, or the one where the competitors get the least in the way.

72 On a broad reach you can boom out your jib. Here Stars 1-5087 and 1-5023 are doing this, during a long leg of the course. But the boat ahead of them, which did not do so, won the race without losing a single inch of its lead.

73 5.5 metres on a run. On this point of sailing, the two ends of the spinnaker must be level to get the best setting for the sail.

74 5.5 metre on a broad reach, on starboard tack. On this point of sailing it is frequently possible to keep up the jib, even though this makes the spinnaker slightly less effective. It is necessary to watch that the speed of the boat is not hindered by keeping up the two sails together.

Beaufort Scale	knots	description
0	< 1	calm
1	1 – 3	light air
2	4 – 6	light breeze
3	7 – 10	gentle breeze
4	11 – 16	moderate breeze
5	17 – 21	fresh breeze
6	22 – 27	strong breeze
7	28 – 33	near gale
8	34 – 40	gale
9	41 – 47	strong gale
10	48 – 55	storm
11	56 – 63	violent storm
12	64 +	hurricane

75 The Mediterranean provides beautiful sailing in blue waters under a blue sky – following in the path of Aeneas and Ulysses.